CONTENTS

Encouraging Interest

Help students to develop an understanding and appreciation for different artists and types of art by highlighting a variety of artists each month. Display examples of an artist's work and have students study and duplicate the style. In addition, encourage students to visit art museums online or visit local art galleries.

Student Sketchbook Ideas

Give each student a large sketchbook in which to explore art techniques, create designs, collect examples of artwork they admire and challenge their thinking about art. Encourage students to add to their sketchbooks at least once a week.

Colouring Pages

These pages are intended to give students practice in using different elements of design.

Rubrics and Checklists

Use the rubrics in this book to assess student learning.

Learning Logs

In addition to a sketchbook have students keep a learning log as an effective way to organize their thoughts and ideas about art concepts presented. Learning logs can include the following kinds of entries:

- teacher journal prompts
- student personal reflections
- questions that arise
- connections discovered
- labelled diagrams

Art Glossary

List new art vocabulary and meanings on chart paper for students' reference during activities.

THE COLOUR WHEEL

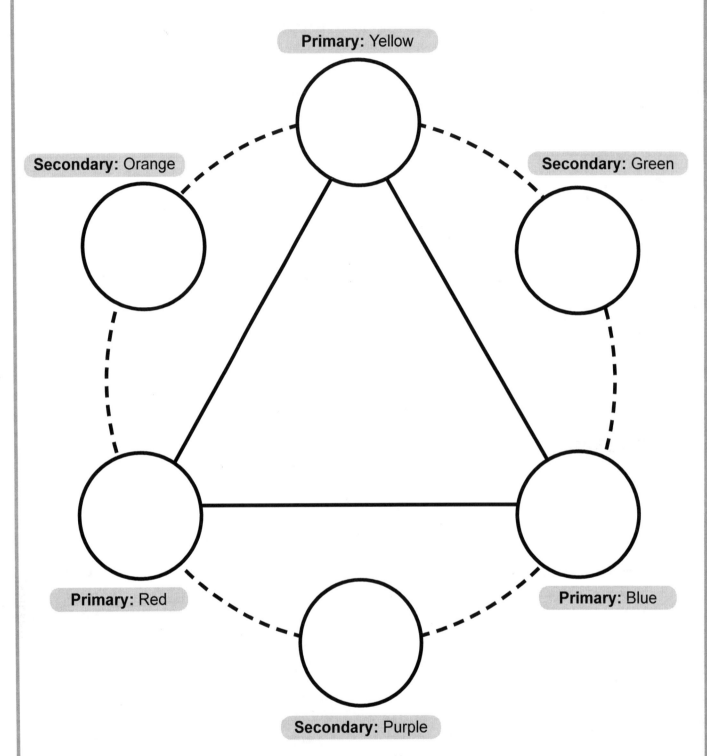

The **primary colours** are red, yellow and blue. Primary colours cannot be mixed or created by any combination of other colours.

The **secondary colours** are purple, green and orange. These colours are created by mixing the primary colours.

What are the primary colours?

_____   _____   _____

Which primary colours make the secondary colours?

 + =

_____   _____   _____

 + =

_____   _____   _____

 + =

_____   _____   _____

Colour the picture using only primary colours. Make sure to colour in the background.

Colour the picture using only secondary colours. Make sure to colour in the background.

CONTRASTING COLOURS

Contrast: A principle of design where light colours are used next to dark colours.

Test different colour combinations on another piece of paper. Then copy the combinations that best match the descriptions below.

STRONGEST CONTRAST

LEAST CONTRAST

FAVOURITE COMBINATIONS

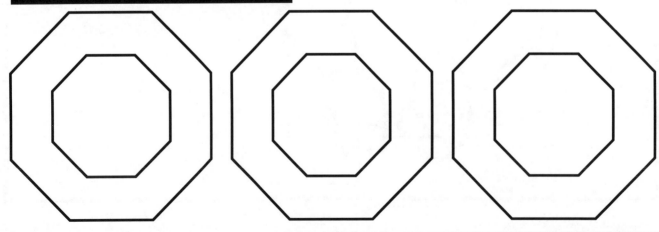

COMPLEMENTARY COLOURS

Complementary colours: Colours opposite each other on the colour wheel. For example: yellow and purple.

Colour the picture using any 2 complementary colours.

ELEMENTS OF DESIGN: VALUE

Shade: Dark value of a colour made by adding black.

Using tempera paint, create shades of the following colours by adding black, a little bit at a time.

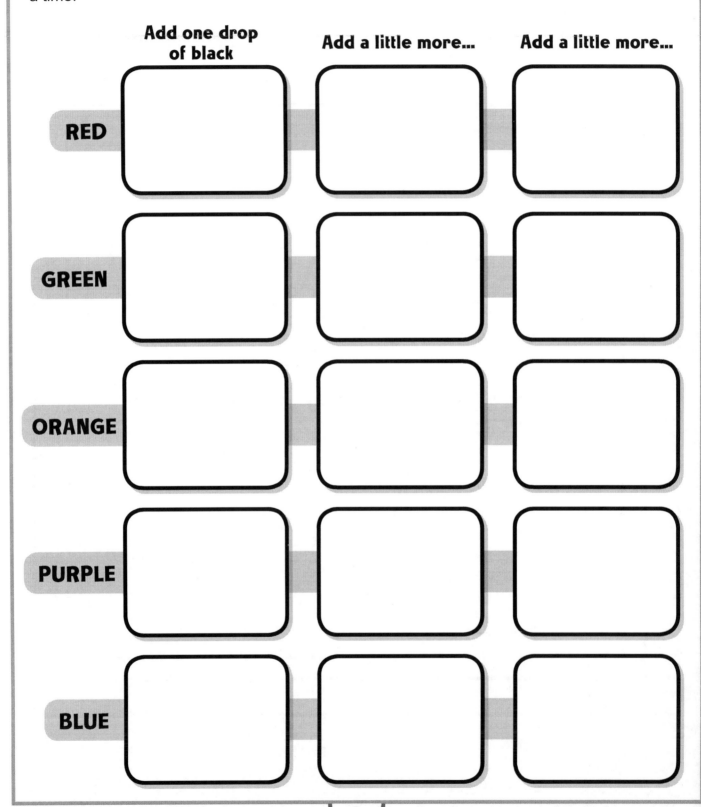

	Add one drop of black	Add a little more...	Add a little more...
RED			
GREEN			
ORANGE			
PURPLE			
BLUE			

8

ELEMENTS OF DESIGN: VALUE

Tint: Light value of a colour made by adding white.

Using tempera paint, create tints of the following colours by adding white, a little bit at a time.

	Add one drop of white	Add a little more...	Add a little more...
RED			
GREEN			
ORANGE			
PURPLE			
BLUE			

9

Monochromatic: Made using different shades and tints of one colour.

Colour each rose in shades or tints of one colour. Choose a different colour for each rose. Make sure to fill in the background for each rose.

Colour the geometric design in different shades of grey.

ELEMENTS OF DESIGN: LINE

Activity 1: Outlining Objects

What you need:

- Crayons
- Pastels
- Paint and paintbrushes
- A variety of everyday objects like scissors, drinking glasses, cans, or toothbrushes
- Paper
- Chalk
- Pencil crayons

What to do:

1. Demonstrate for students how to trace the contour of various objects to create a pleasing line composition.

2. Invite students to trace various objects and overlap them to create their own line compositions. Encourage students to use assorted drawing materials and colours and to notice the types of lines created by each.

Activity 2: Contour Drawing

What you need:

- Paper   • Small fruits   • HB pencil

What to do:

1. Explain to students that they will be completing a contour drawing of a small fruit such as a pear or banana. Review the term contour drawing.

2. Have students begin by placing the fruit of their choice near the paper. Students may find it helpful to strive to make their drawings the same size as the actual fruit.

3. Then encourage students to begin their contour drawing. They should choose a point on the edge of the fruit and follow its contour with their eyes, allowing their hand to copy the shape of the fruit onto the paper.

4. Caution students not to rush. They should try to draw every curve, including strong lines on the fruit such as a fold or crease.

5. Remind students that the purpose of this activity is to practise getting their hand and eye to do the same thing, by judging the size and shape of the edges the student can see.

6. Once done, have students review their drawings and consider whether their drawings match the real-life shapes of the fruit. Discuss whether the proportions are correct and whether enough details were included.

7. Repeat this drawing activity using different everyday objects.

12

ELEMENTS OF DESIGN: LINE

Activity 3: Rhythm and Line

What you need:

- Crayons
- Pastels
- Different types of music
- Paper
- Chalk
- Pencil crayons

What to do:

1. Choose and play a piece of music for students and have them trace the rhythm of the music with a finger in the air. Ask them to describe the line their finger creates.

2. Now have students draw the line that represents the rhythm of the music using the material(s) and colour(s) of their choice. Have students add more such lines above and below the first line.

3. Repeat the activity with different types of music and discuss as a class why students chose the types of lines and colours they did.

Activity 4: Sgraffito

What you need:

- Paper (untextured)
- Crayons
- Paintbrushes
- Thick tempera paint
- Objects that scratch, such as, toothpicks, tongue depressors, combs, coins and plastic utensils

What to do:

1. Invite students to draw broad bands of colour, using crayons, on a piece of paper that has a smooth surface. Remind students to apply pressure on the crayons as they draw.

2. Once completed, have students paint over the entire paper with the black tempera paint.

3. After the paint dries encourage students to scratch designs onto the paper using the objects. This technique is called sgraffito.

Draw examples of the following lines.

Thin Lines

Thick Lines

Wavy Lines

Dotted Lines

Zigzag Lines

Horizontal Lines

Diagonal Lines

Vertical Lines

Using pencil crayons, fill in the sections of the picture by using different types of coloured lines.

Using pencil crayons, fill in the sections of the picture by using different types of coloured lines.

Fill in the sections of the picture by using different types of lines. Then, add a colourful patterned background.

ELEMENTS OF DESIGN: FORM

Activity 1: Drawing People

What you need:

• White paper • Pencil and eraser • Colouring materials

What to do:

1. Demonstrate for students how the human body may be looked upon as a series of connected oval or sausage-like shapes.

2. Use a student as a model to draw, and help students see the breakdown of the oval body parts.

3. Once you have drawn all of the oval segments of the human form, erase the overlapping lines where body parts connect. Point out to students that there are joints where many body parts connect. Joints include the shoulders, knees and wrists.

4. Next, add clothing and other features to complete the drawing. Show students how to add lines to the area around joints to show bent limbs and creases.

5. Students are now ready to draw their humans. Have students work in pairs, so that they can be models for each other. Encourage students to draw their partners in various positions.

Activity 2: Animated People

What you need:

• White paper • Pencil and eraser • Colouring materials

What to do:

1. Review with students how the human body may be looked upon as a series of connected oval or sausage-like shapes.

2. Next, have students work in pairs. One partner will pose while the other partner will draw the partner in a series of 3–5 positions that show action, such as when participating in a sport.

3. Encourage students to draw details on their animated person and facial expressions.

4. Students should also add a background to their picture.

Chalkboard Publishing © 2012

SCULPTURE FUN

Give students opportunities to sculpt and paint different forms. In addition to dough (see recipes below), provide students with cookie cutters, rollers, plastic knives, plastic spoons, and wooden craft sticks as well as paints and paintbrushes. Demonstrate for students how to roll, flatten, and pinch dough to form shapes. You may also provide students with wiggle eyes, buttons, and pipe cleaners to add to their sculptures. Store dough in sealed containers.

Self-Hardening Dough

- 1 1/2 cups water
- 1 1/2 cups salt
- 4 cups flour
- 1 teaspoon alum

1. Mix dry ingredients in a bowl.
2. Gradually add water.
3. Knead until the mixture is pliable.

Sand Sculpture Dough

- 4 cups clean sand (not beach sand)
- 2 cups cornstarch
- 2 cups water

1. Mix all ingredients in a saucepan.
2. Heat the mixture over medium heat and stir until it becomes as thick as modelling clay.
3. Once the mixture is the right consistency, allow it to cool before handling.

Smelly Modelling Dough

- 3 cups flour
- 1/2 cup salt
- 2 packages flavoured drink crystals
- 2 cups boiling water

1. Mix dry ingredients in a bowl.
2. Add boiling water.
3. Mix and knead on a floured surface.

Draw the other half of the picture. Colour the picture.

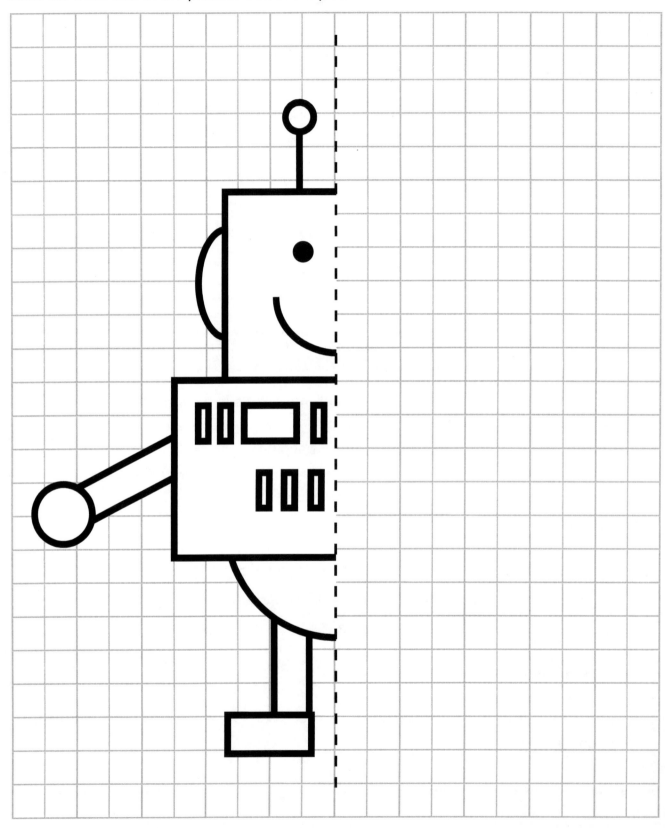

ORIGAMI DOLL

What you need:

• A square piece of white paper   • Colouring materials

What to do:

1.
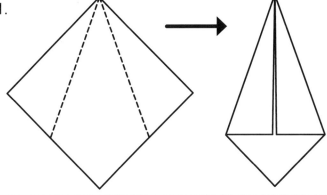
Demonstrate for students how to fold two edges of the square to the centre line to form a diamond shape.

2.

Next, show students how to fold the triangle at the bottom up.

3.

Now, make a fold near the centre of the triangle, bringing the bottom part up over the top part.

4.
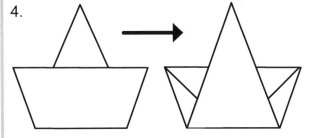
Then, demonstrate how to flip the entire origami piece over.

5.

Lastly, show students how to fold each of the two triangular flaps toward the centre. These will be the doll's arms.

6.

Encourage students to draw and colour a face, hair, clothes, hands and other details.

Use these body parts to draw your own fantasy creature.

BRAIN STRETCH: On a separate piece of paper, create your own fantasy creature.

22

ELEMENTS OF DESIGN: TEXTURE

Activity 1: Fruit and Veggie Printmaking

What you need:

- Cut sections of a variety of fruit and vegetables
- Styrofoam plates
- Tempera paint in assorted colours
- Paper

What to do:

1. Pour tempera paint onto Styrofoam plates, one colour per plate.

2. Demonstrate for students how to carefully press cut sections of vegetables or fruit into the paint and then press those paint-laden sections onto paper to create a print. Remind students not to drag the fruit or vegetable across the page.

3. Encourage students to create patterns or designs with one or more sections of fruit or vegetable.

4. Invite students to share and discuss their prints with each other. How did they create different patterns? Which fruits or vegetables produced the best prints?

Activity 2: Monoprints

What you need:

- Printmaking ink or tempera paint with flour added to make its consistency thicker
- Paintbrushes
- Small sheets of Plexiglas
- Paper
- A covered work area

What to do:

1. Tell students that monoprints are unique: only one print is made from the printing plate.

2. Demonstrate for students how to paint a design or picture onto the Plexiglas. Emphasize that students must work quickly so that the paint won't dry.

3. Next, show students how to place the paper over the Plexiglas and press lightly with the palm of the hand, to transfer the design onto the paper.

4. Peel away the paper and admire the monoprint!

23

EXPERIMENT WITH TEXTURE

Encourage students to create different textures with the tools, materials, and papers listed below. They can use the textures to create a collage or to fill sections of a picture.

Out-of-the-Ordinary Painting Tools

- Fingers
- Sticks
- Blocks of wood
- Branches
- Rope
- Feathers
- Leaves
- Sponges
- Tissues
- Brushes
- Cotton swabs
- Cotton balls
- Plastic pot scrubbers
- Plastic wrap
- Makeup brushes

Excellent Drawing and Painting Materials

- Crayons
- Pencils
- Pastels
- Chalk
- Charcoal
- Ink pen
- Water-based markers
- Acrylic paint
- Makeup
- Tempera paint
- Felt tip pens
- Pencil crayons
- Watercolours
- Food colouring

A Variety of Surfaces on Which to Paint or Draw

- Newsprint
- Paper plates
- Blocks of wood
- Tissue paper
- Paper bags
- Sandpaper
- Wet paper
- Cardboard
- Fabric
- Plastic wrap
- Paper towels
- Waxed paper
- Aluminum foil
- Stones
- Foam

CREATE DIFFERENT TEXTURES

Corn Syrup Paint

Make a striking paint with an interesting texture by combining food colouring and light corn syrup. Mix up as many colours as needed. Encourage students to paint different landscapes or oceanscapes. Students may wish to first create an outline drawing with a permanent marker before painting. Be sure to allow more than a day of drying time.

Flour-and-Water Fingerpaint

This paint will help you to achieve great textures when finger painting. Mix 1 cup flour, 1 cup water and 2 teaspoons salt in a small container to make a paint with the consistency of thick gravy. Add in the desired food colouring. Repeat the process for as many colours as needed.

Glossy Paint

Give tempera paint a wet, glossy look by combining 1 part white glue and 1 part tempera paint.

Puff Paint

Have students create unique pictures using puff paint. Combine 1 cup salt, 1 cup sugar and the desired food colouring in a squeeze bottle. Shake the ingredients and squeeze the paint out of the bottle onto the paper.

Sand Paint

Sand paint offers an interesting option when striving to create texture in a picture. Begin by having students create a simple outline drawing. Then make the sand paint by combining 1 part sand and 5 parts powdered tempera. Encourage students to experiment when mixing the sand and tempera to achieve the desired colour. Next, when a few sand paint colours have been made, use a wooden craft stick to spread a thin layer of glue in one section of the outline drawing. Then, using a spoon, gently pour the sand paint into the glue-covered section. Lightly lift the paper to shake off any excess sand paint. Allow the sand painting to dry, and seal it using hairspray.

Wax Resist

As wax and water don't mix, the wax resist technique can be used to mask out areas to preserve the white of the paper or the colour beneath and to create appealing textures. Draw or colour with a wax crayon and then wash over it with a water-based paint.

Pointillism: A technique of painting in which tiny dots of colour are placed close together. From a distance, the dots seem to disappear and the colours blend.

Fill in sections of the landscape using only small dots of colour. Use markers.

EXPLORING TEXTURE

Fill in sections of the picture by pasting torn bits of coloured construction paper.

BRAIN STRETCH: Draw the outline of a new picture with a black marker and fill it in the same way.

Paint the landscape at sunset using watercolours.

Colour the landscape using oil pastels and set it with hairspray.

EXPLORING TEXTURE

Fill in sections of the landscape using different colours of Plasticine. Paint the sky using sunset colours.

Fill in sections of the picture using different textures.

ELEMENTS OF DESIGN: SPACE

Activity 1: Focal Point of a Composition

What you need:

- Colouring materials, such as oil pastels, pencil crayons or crayons
- Large sheets of paper
- Students' favourite stuffed animals or toys

What to do:

1. Discuss with students the concept of a focal point in a composition. The focal point draws a viewer's eye first. Explain how objects that are smaller than the focal point appear to be farther away from the viewer.

2. Instruct students to begin a composition by drawing their stuffed animal or toy and making it the focal point. Tell students that their stuffed animal should be as tall as a ruler.

3. Next, have students add a background to their composition. They should add a horizon line and objects that are farther away (and so smaller). Students can brainstorm possible locations for the stuffed animal (e.g., bedroom, forest) and think about the details of the location they choose.

4. Have students colour their completed composition. Encourage students not to leave any blank areas.

Activity 2: Fill In the Missing Pieces

What you need:

- A picture cut from a magazine or calendar (e.g., car, flower, nature scene)
- Thick, white paper the same size as the magazine or calendar cutout
- Scissors
- Glue
- Crayons, coloured pencils or oil pastels

What to do:

1. First, demonstrate for students how to cut their picture into wide diagonal strips.

2. Next, show students how to glue half of the picture strips onto the white paper, positioning every other piece where it would be if the picture were in one piece but leaving lots of space between the strips.

3. Then, have students draw and colour in the missing sections of the picture, using the media of their choice. Students can use their imagination or common sense to fill in the missing sections.

ELEMENTS OF DESIGN: SPACE

Activity 3: Landscape

What you need:

• White paper   • Oil pastels   • Cotton balls for smudging

What to do:

1. Review with students the art terms foreground, middle ground and background and tell students that they will be painting a landscape. Look at and discuss examples of landscapes.

2. To begin, show students how to lightly sketch with their pencil these three sections using ground, water and ground.

3. Instruct students to fill each section with paint. Encourage students to mix colours and to use more than one shade or tint of colour.

4. Once the sections are completely covered with paint, have students add details and objects to the sections using darker colours. Remind students that objects in the foreground are the most prominent and appear to be the closest to the viewer. Alternatively, objects that are smaller are intended to appear farther away from the viewer.

Activity 4: Streetscape in One-Point Perspective

What you need:

• Colouring materials   • Pencil   • Eraser   • Ruler

What to do:

1. Review with students the art terms perspective, horizon line and vanishing point. Show examples of each term and how they are used in artwork.

2. Explain to students that they will draw a streetscape in one-point perspective. Have students begin by drawing a horizon line on their papers.

3. Next, students should find the midpoint of the horizon line and mark it as the vanishing point for their drawing.

4. Demonstrate for students how to mark the bottom right and left corners of their paper and then draw a line from each mark to the vanishing point. This will create the illusion of a street.

5. Have students add three-dimensional buildings along each side of the street. Remind students that buildings should decrease in size as they approach the vanishing point.

6. Encourage students to add other details to their drawings, both along the street and along the horizon line.

Complete the picture by adding a horizon line and vanishing point. Add details to the picture and colour it.

ELEMENTS OF DESIGN: SHAPE

Activity 1: Shape Picture

What you need:

• Black construction paper • Scissors • Shape cutouts • Glue • Colouring materials

What to do:

1. Ask students to plan and compose a picture using their choice of shape cutouts on a black background. Have available white and coloured cutouts of geometric shapes. (You will find outlines of some geometric shapes on the following pages.) Possible subjects for students' pictures include animals, buildings, nature, people or inventions.

2. Once students have planned a detailed composition, have them glue the shapes onto the black construction paper. Encourage students to use a specific colour scheme. Offer different media for colouring or adding designs to white cutouts.

Note: You may wish to demonstrate ways to use different shapes, for example, using heart shapes for an animal's feet.

Activity 2: Shape Collage

What you need:

• Paper
• Watercolours
• Paintbrushes

• Rulers
• Black markers
• Pencils

What to do:

1. Instruct students to produce a design of black outlines of overlapping geometric shapes. Encourage students to use a variety of shapes in their design.

2. Next, have students paint sections of the design using a specific approach, such as complementary colours only, secondary colours only, different tints, and so on.

3. When students have finished, discuss with them their approach to their artwork.

Chalkboard Publishing © 2012

SHAPE HUNT

Find and list places where you see or use the following geometric shapes in everyday life.

Circle ○	**Octagon** ⬡

Triangle △	**Trapezoid** ▢

Square ▢	**Hexagon** ⬡

Rectangle ▭	**Oval** ⬭

ORGANIC SHAPE HUNT

Organic Shape: Non-geometric or free-flowing shapes, such as a cloud or a leaf.

Look around you and draw different organic shapes you see.

HOW TO DRAW A DOG

Step 1

Step 2

Step 3

Step 4

HOW TO DRAW A CAT

Step 1

Step 2

Step 3

Step 4

GEOMETRIC SHAPE OUTLINES

Chalkboard Publishing © 2012

42

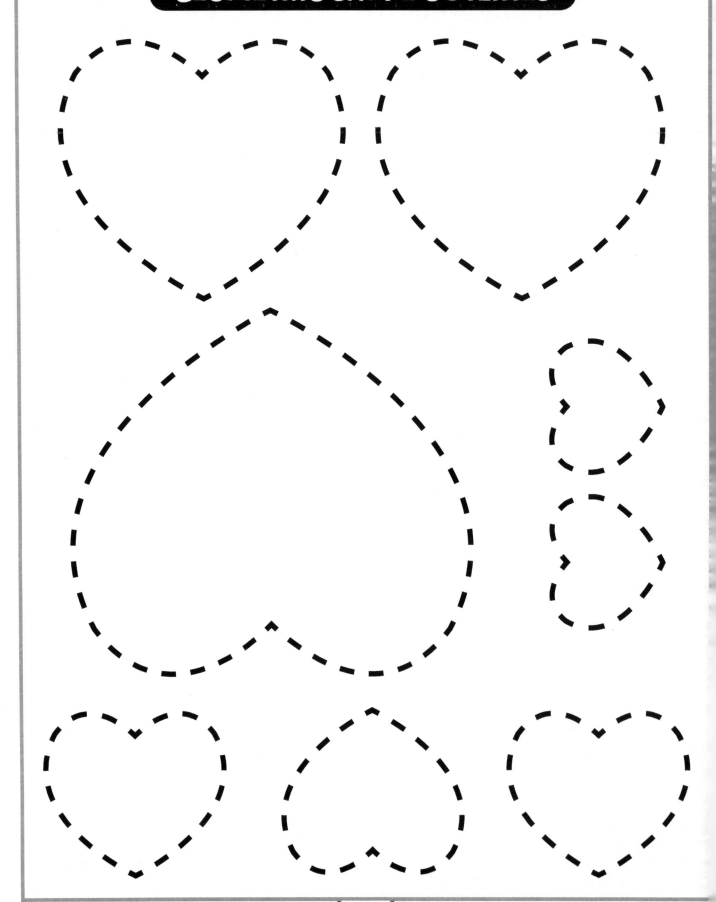

Complete the picture using different elements of design. On a separate piece of paper, explain how you used the elements.

Complete the picture using different elements of design. On a separate piece of paper, explain how you used the elements.

Complete the picture using different elements of design. On a separate piece of paper, explain how you used the elements.

Complete the picture using different elements of design. On a separate piece of paper, explain how you used the elements.

Complete the picture using different elements of design. On a separate piece of paper, explain how you used the elements.

51

EXPERIMENTING WITH ELEMENTS OF DESIGN

Complete the picture using different elements of design. Make sure you add details to the background. On a separate piece of paper, explain how you used the elements.

EXPERIMENTING WITH ELEMENTS OF DESIGN

Complete the picture using different elements of design. Make sure you add details to the background. On a separate piece of paper, explain how you used the elements.

Complete the picture using different elements of design. Make sure you add details to the background. On a separate piece of paper, explain how you used the elements.

DRAW A PORTRAIT

Draw a family member, friend or pet.

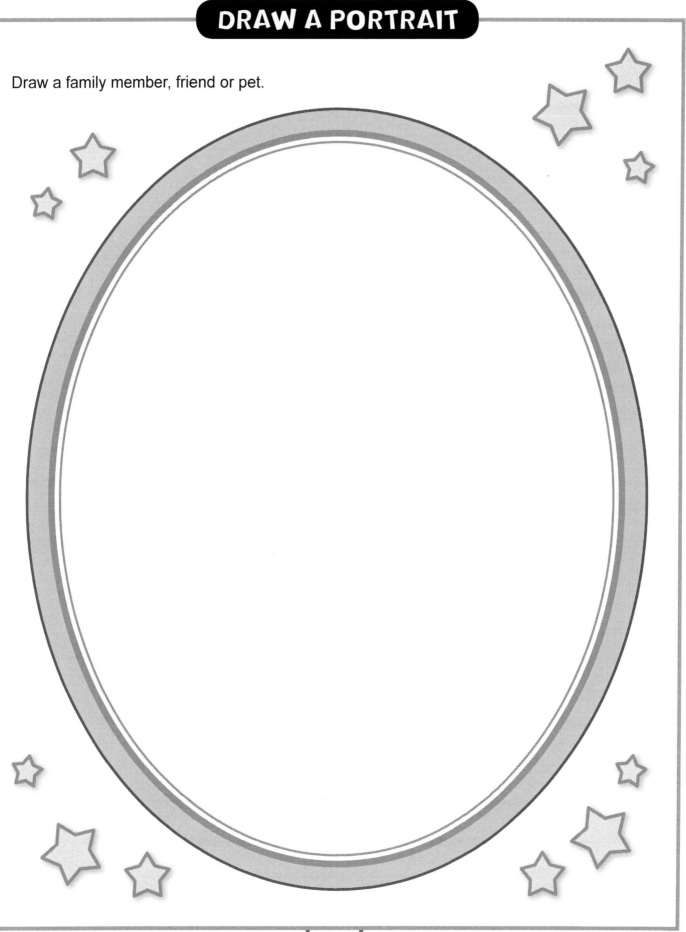

Create a picture using images cut out of old magazines.

Create your own coat of arms.

Create a stamp.

Write about your stamp:

_____

_____

_____

DISCUSSION PROMPTS: LOOKING AT A PAINTING

Description

- Describe the subject of the painting.
- What colours do you see?
- What shapes do you see?
- What textures do you see?
- What kind of lines do you see?
- What kind of objects do you see?
- What kind of forms do you see?

Analysis

- What is the focal point of the painting?
- Is there an element of design that is most prominent in the painting? Explain.
- Do you think the composition is balanced? Explain.
- Does the artist show movement in the painting? If so, how?
- Does the painting have a sense of three dimensions?
- What angle of view do you think the artist had when painting this subject? Explain your thinking.

Interpretation

- What kind of mood do you think the artist is trying to encourage when viewing the painting?
- How does the painting make you feel?
- What message or meaning do you think the artist is trying to convey?
- Why do you think the artist chose to paint this particular subject?

Personal Opinion

- Do you like the painting? Why or why not?
- What, if anything, does this painting remind you of? Explain.
- The painting is a good example of … or The painting is a bad example of …
- Do you think the title of the painting is a good one? Explain.
- Would you like to see more paintings from this artist? Why or why not?
- Would you buy this painting? Why or why not?

Chalkboard Publishing © 2012

CANADIAN-INSPIRED ART IDEAS

Aboriginal Snowshoes

What you need:

- Hole punch
- Pencil
- Scissors
- Heavy cardboard
- Sturdy yarn or twine

What to do:

1. Discuss with students how Aboriginal peoples introduced snowshoes to early Canadian settlers and tell students they will be making their own pair.
2. Begin by giving each student two pieces of the heavy cardboard to act as the base of the snowshoes.
3. Have students work in pairs to trace the outline of their partner's foot as he or she stands on the heavy cardboard.
4. Next, have each student draw a large oval around the outline of each foot. The oval should extend at least 20 cm.
5. Then, demonstrate for students how to carefully cut out the oval shapes.
6. Once the oval shapes are ready, have student punch out holes on opposite sides of the arch area.
7. Using sturdy yarn or twine, demonstrate for students how to lace each "snowshoe."
8. When finished, have students try out their "snowshoes," by lacing them up and walking around the room.

Canadian Collage

What you need:

- Glue
- Scissors
- White paper
- Magazine pictures
- Canadian travel brochures

What to do:

1. Have students look through magazines and Canadian travel brochures to find and cut out pictures related to a theme. Themes may include Canadian animals, different Canadian landscapes, Canadian urban settings, Canadian rural settings or Canadian symbols.
2. Once students have cut out the various pictures related to their theme, have students arrange them into a collage and paste them onto their paper.

Chalkboard Publishing © 2012

CANADIAN-INSPIRED ART IDEAS

Canada's Aurora Borealis

What you need:

• Small pieces of black construction paper   • Red and green tempera paint   • Glitter

What to do:

1. Show students pictures of Canada's famous northern lights, or aurora borealis, which can be seen in Canada's north.
2. Using a plastic spoon, demonstrate for students how to lightly drip red and green paint onto the black construction paper.
3. Next, have students place a second piece of black construction paper on top of the first piece of black construction paper.
4. Instruct students to twist the second piece of black construction paper with their hand so that the dripped paint underneath blends into the form of a band of red and green colours.
5. Then have students pull the papers apart and sprinkle glitter along the band of blended colours to resemble Canada's aurora borealis.

Canadian Forest Landscape

What you need:

• Blue construction paper
• Magazine pictures of Canadian animals
• Glue
• Green tissue paper in a variety of shades
• Brown construction paper in a variety of shades

What to do:

1. Show students examples of real Canadian forest landscapes. Then share examples of landscapes painted by the Group of Seven.
2. Begin by demonstrating for students how to tear different lengths of tree trunks from brown construction paper. Encourage children to add branches to their tree trunks.
3. Next, instruct students to glue the tree trunks and branches onto the blue paper. Remind students how smaller trees look like they are located farther away.
4. Then, tear different green shades of tissue paper into small pieces for leaves.
5. Next, students can paste the tissue paper leaves onto the tree branches and the forest floor.
6. Encourage students to paste magazine cutouts of Canadian forest animals onto their picture for more detail.

INUKSHUK

An Inukshuk is a stone marker. It can show the way or convey a message. Some inukshuks look like people. Make your own inukshuk by tearing and pasting grey construction paper.

Design a Canadian Olympic $1 coin.

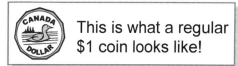

This is what a regular $1 coin looks like!

The Canadian $1 coin is nicknamed the "loonie" because of the loon in the design. Think of and explain a nickname for your Olympic coin.

_____

_____

Colour Canada's coat of arms.

SIMILARITIES AND DIFFERENCES

Describe two artworks.

Artist and description of artwork	Artist and description of artwork

Compare

How are the artworks **similar**?

Contrast

How are the artworks **different**?

DIRECT DRAW

Encourage students to think of art as the personal interpretation of ideas. This quick activity demonstrates how students given the same directions will each produce a unique artwork. Collect and display all of the students' completed artworks. You will have a wonderful collection of abstract art based on shape, colour and line.

WHAT YOU NEED:

- Square piece of paper
- Colouring materials

WHAT TO DO:

1. Tell students that they will each complete a piece of art by following your oral directions. Before you begin, ask students to predict whether or not all the students' works will look the same.

2. Give each student the same materials.

3. Call out directions. For example:

   - Draw a thin line across the page.

   - Draw a thick line across the page.

   - Draw a circle anywhere on the page.

   - Draw a triangle somewhere on the page.

   - ...

   Add directions of your choice that will reinforce art vocabulary. Give students enough time to follow each direction before calling out the next one.

4. When all the directions have been called out, have students compare and contrast their artworks with a partner. How are the pieces the same? How are they different?

5. Display the students' artworks.

SKETCHBOOK DRAWING IDEAS

Portrait

- Draw a self-portrait. Look at yourself in a mirror for reference.
- Draw a self-portrait of yourself 50 years from now.
- Draw a portrait of a friend or family member.
- Draw a portrait of your favourite stuffed animal.
- Draw a portrait of your pet.
- Draw a portrait of your favourite cartoon character.

Still Life

- Draw a beautiful flower arrangement.
- Draw a plant with attention to detail.
- Draw a piece of fruit.
- Draw a piece of furniture with attention to colour, shading and textures.
- Draw a favourite toy.
- Draw a bowl of fruit.
- Draw an arrangement of 3D figures with attention to shading.

Design

- Design a CD cover for your favourite group or singer.
- Design a logo for your class.
- Design a new cover for a book.
- Design an advertisement for a special event.
- Design a poster for your favourite movie.
- Design the can for a new drink.
- Design the outside of your dream house.
- Design a new invention.
- Design a new Canadian stamp.
- Design a new Canadian coin.
- Design a new outfit.
- Design a car.
- Design a new Canadian flag.
- Design a castle.

Other

- Draw a scene from another planet.
- Draw a giant looking down at a village.
- Draw a new creature.
- Draw an alien.
- Draw an airplane.
- Draw a spaceship.
- Draw what you see outside your bedroom window.
- Draw a boat.
- Draw what the world looked like during the time of the dinosaurs.

FALL

- Paint a fall mural on the classroom windows using a mixture of equal parts dishwashing liquid and paint (use washable liquid paint or powdered tempera paint). Encourage students to add as many details as possible.

- Make paper ears of corn. Students cut long ear-of-corn shapes from yellow construction paper. Instruct students to glue down small squares of yellow, orange and brown tissue paper to represent the kernels. When the glue is dry, add brown construction paper in the shape of the husk to the back.

- Sketch a still life of a cornucopia.

- Make leaf rubbings. Students should bring in fall leaves in all shapes and sizes and arrange them on paper. Students place another piece of paper on top and use chalk or crayons to make different types of rubbings.

- Use the shape outline cutouts in this resource to assemble shape pictures of a Halloween cat, witch, haunted house or bat. Students can paint the shapes using a textured paint and glue them onto black construction paper.

- Paint a spooky, black-and-orange Halloween picture.

- Assemble pasta skeletons. Provide students with different-shaped pieces of pasta and black construction paper. Students should glue the pasta pieces down once they are pleased with their arrangement.

- Produce beautiful "stained glass" Christmas windows using black construction paper and tissue paper. Students cut out Christmas symbols from the black construction paper, leaving the "window frame." Then students carefully paste different colours of tissue paper to create a stained glass effect.

- Construct three-dimensional Christmas trees. First, tell students to fold two rectangular pieces of green construction paper in half. Then, show students how to do the following: draw half a Christmas tree opposite the fold on one piece of paper, place the folded pieces of paper one on top of the other, and cut along the outline of the tree to produce two identical, symmetrical tree shapes. Cut a slit along the crease in the centre of the bottom half of one tree and the top half of the other tree. Fit the two shapes together.

WINTER

- Paint a winter mural on the classroom windows using a mixture of equal parts dishwashing liquid and paint (use washable liquid paint or powdered tempera paint).

- Draw a winter scene using crayons and apply a wash with salt added, for a snowy effect.

- Draw people in motion participating in various winter sports and activities.

- Make Valentine's Day pendants using self-hardening clay. Students can mould their own shape or use cookie cutters as guides. Paint the pendants with acrylic paint once the clay is dry.

- Weave a paper heart. Model for students how to fold a piece of red or pink construction paper exactly in half. Then, using a pencil, draw the outline of half a heart opposite the fold and cut along the outline to create a heart shape. Demonstrate for students how to carefully cut long slits parallel to the fold without cutting the heart into pieces. Then show them how to weave strips of white, red and pink paper through the heart.

- Create a shamrock crown. Students cut shamrock shapes in different sizes and sponge paint them in different tints and shades of green. Once the shamrocks are dry, students paste them onto a strip of green construction paper. Staple the strip to fit each student's head. Students could also add glitter to their crowns.

- Go outside on a snowy day and create snow sculptures!

- Make glossy snowflakes. Students cut snowflakes out of aluminum foil and carefully paste white tissue paper behind them. Display the snowflakes on a window.

Chalkboard Publishing © 2012

SPRING

- Paint a spring mural on the classroom windows using a mixture of equal parts dishwashing liquid and paint (use washable liquid paint or powdered tempera paint).

- Create seed mosaics using the shape outlines in this book as a base.

- Use papier-mâché to decorate old vases in spring colours. Students can plant a flower in the vase (or fill it with paper flowers) and give it as a Mother's Day gift.

- Decorate the classroom with gorgeous spring blossoms. First, students paint brown branches on white paper. When the paint is dry, they add tissue paper blossoms as follows: wrap small squares of tissue paper around the end of a pencil, dab on a small amount of glue, and paste each square onto a branch.

- Use oil pastels to draw and colour realistic pictures of spring flowers or insects. Students should use close-up photographs as references. Set students' pictures with hairspray.

- Draw a still life of an Easter lily arrangement

- Design an Earth Day stamp or commemorative coin.

- Create an Earth Day collage using cutouts from old magazines and other print media.

- Decorate paper Easter eggs. Students cut egg shapes out of construction paper and draw line patterns on them with water-based markers. Students can trace over the marker lines with white glue to produce an embossed effect (the glue will dry clear).

- Produce beautiful insect and flower "stained glass" windows using black construction paper and tissue paper. Students cut out the desired shapes from the black construction paper, leaving the "window frame." Then students carefully paste different colours of tissue paper to create a stained glass effect.

- Make colourful paper-bag birds. Students start by cutting feathers of different shapes and sizes from construction paper. Demonstrate how to place and glue the feathers around the bag, starting from the back. Encourage students to create a pattern of colour. Students can add triangle-shaped wings covered in feathers, eyes and a beak.

- Paint a summer mural on the classroom windows using a mixture of equal parts dishwashing liquid and paint (use washable liquid paint or powdered tempera paint).

- Make miniature kites. Use straws or wooden craft sticks to construct the frame and cover it with tissue paper. Attach string.

- Create beautiful tissue paper flowers. Students take four to six rectangular pieces of tissue paper and fold them as a pile into an accordion. Next, they tie the centre of the pile with a twist tie. Demonstrate for students how to carefully pull each piece of tissue paper up toward the centre of the flower, so that the pieces of tissue paper are separated to form petals. Finally, add a stem using a green pipe cleaner or Bristol board.

- Celebrate Canada Day. Design a stamp using the blackline master in this resource and/ or create a diorama depicting all things Canadian.

- Turn a rock into a paperweight and give it as a gift for Father's Day. Invite students to bring rocks to class and to decorate the rock of their choice with acrylic paint.

- Draw the outline of a summer scene and fill sections of the drawing using mixed media.

- Draw a still life of beach toys, your favourite place to visit during the summer or a bicycle.

- Use oil pastels to draw a still life of a bowl of fruit.

- Build a sandcastle using sand clay. Once the sandcastle is finished, students should gently pat dry sand on the moist clay.

- Create a diorama of a summer garden or a beach scene.

- Design and create a mixed-media poster of the ultimate vacation spot. Students can use magazine pictures of places they would like to visit for inspiration and reference.

- Assemble two-dimensional paper flowers with stems and leaves. Students can arrange cutout shapes (from the shape outline blackline masters in this resource) on a coloured piece of construction paper and fill in each shape with a textured paint.

ART RUBRICS

UNDERSTANDING OF ART CONCEPTS RUBRIC

LEVEL	DESCRIPTORS
4	Student shows a thorough understanding of all or almost all concepts and consistently gives appropriate and complete explanations independently. No teacher support is needed.
3	Student shows a good understanding of most concepts and usually gives complete or nearly complete explanations. Infrequent teacher support is needed.
2	Student shows a satisfactory understanding of most concepts and sometimes gives appropriate, but incomplete, explanations. Teacher support is sometimes needed.
1	Student shows little understanding of concepts and rarely gives complete explanations. Intensive teacher support is needed.

COMMUNICATION OF CONCEPTS RUBRIC

LEVEL	DESCRIPTORS
4	Student almost always uses correct art terminology with clarity and precision during class discussions.
3	Student frequently uses correct art terminology during class discussions.
2	Student occasionally uses correct art terminology during class discussions.
1	Student rarely uses correct art terminology during class discussions.

ANALYSIS OF ARTWORKS RUBRIC

LEVEL	DESCRIPTORS
4	Student accurately describes several dominant elements or principles used by the artist. Student accurately describes how they are used by the artist to reinforce the theme, meaning, mood or feeling of the artwork.
3	Student describes without assistance most of the dominant elements and principles used by the artist. Student describes without assistance how these relate to the meaning, mood, theme or feeling of the artwork.
2	Student describes with little assistance some dominant elements and principles used by the artist. Student needs some teacher prompts to describe how these relate to the meaning, mood, theme or feeling of the artwork.
1	Student has difficulty describing the dominant elements and principles used by the artist in the artwork without direct teacher prompts.

INTERPRETATION OF ARTWORKS RUBRIC

LEVEL	DESCRIPTORS
4	Student analyzes and interprets the meaning of the artwork independently using extensive evidence from the artwork.
3	Student analyzes and interprets the meaning of the artwork with occasional teacher prompts using satisfactory evidence from the artwork.
2	Student requires some teacher prompts to analyze and interpret the meaning of the artwork.
1	Student requires direct teacher assistance to analyze and interpret the meaning of the artwork.

CREATIVE WORK RUBRIC

LEVEL	DESCRIPTORS
4	Student applies almost all of the skills, techniques and art concepts taught.
3	Student applies most of the skills, techniques and art concepts taught.
2	Student applies more than half of the skills, techniques and art concepts taught.
1	Student applies fewer than half of the skills, techniques and art concepts taught.

PARTICIPATION RUBRIC

LEVEL	DESCRIPTORS
4	Student consistently contributes to class discussions and activities by offering ideas and asking questions.
3	Student usually contributes to class discussions and activities by offering ideas and asking questions.
2	Student sometimes contributes to class discussions and activities by offering ideas and asking questions.
1	Student rarely contributes to class discussions and activities by offering ideas and asking questions.

CLASS EVALUATION LIST

Student Name	Class Participation	Understanding of Concepts	Communication of Concepts	Analysis of Artworks	Interpretation of Artworks	Creative Work	Overall Evaluation

ART WEBSITES FOR STUDENTS

Hello Kids

http://www.hellokids.com

Have students visit the "Drawing" section of this fantastic site. Here students will find several easy-to-follow, step-by-step instructions for drawing a variety of animals and characters.

Learn About Color

http://www.metmuseum.org/metmedia/interactives/start-with-art/learn-about-color

Here, students can mix colours and watch as a labelled colour wheel is assembled.

McMichael Canadian Art Collection

http://www.mcmichael.com

This important Canadian gallery houses a permanent collection of almost 6000 artworks by Tom Thomson, the Group of Seven and their contemporaries, as well as First Nations, Inuit and other artists who have made a contribution to Canada's artistic heritage. Teachers and students can view and research objects in the collection online.

Artists in Canada

http://www.artistsincanada.com

A comprehensive national directory of Canadian artists, art galleries and art resources.

The National Gallery of Canada

http://www.gallery.ca

Click on "Learn" to view online exhibitions and to access special interactive features for kids and teens. Themed lesson plans are also available in this part of the website. Each lesson plan includes activities for students at different grade levels.

Build Your Wild Self

http://buildyourwildself.com

This is a great website where students can design a digital human and add animal characteristics.

ART GLOSSARY

Abstract art: Art that uses lines, shapes, colours and textures to portray a realistic object in a non-realistic, imaginary way.

Allegory: The use of symbolic figures to represent abstract ideas such as honour and sacrifice.

Analogous colours: Two or more colours that are next to each other on the colour wheel. For example: red, red-orange and orange.

Background: The part of the picture plane that seems to be farthest from the viewer.

Balance: A principle of design that deals with arranging the visual elements in a work of art for harmony of design and proportion.

Cast shadow: The shadow created on a surface when an objects blocks the light.

Complementary colours: Colours opposite each other on the colour wheel. For example: yellow and purple.

Collage: Creating a picture by gluing pieces of materials such as paper, photos, magazine clippings or found objects to a flat surface.

Colour: Colour is an element of design. Eyes see colour when light bounces off an object. The four characteristics of colour are hue, saturation, value and temperature.

Colour wheel: A tool for creating and organizing colours and representing relationships among colours.

Comic: A graphic art form in which images and words are used to tell a story. The images are the main focus and are usually presented in strip or page layout.

Composition: Describes the organization of the elements of design used in an artwork.

Contemporary art: Art created by living artists.

Contour drawing: An outline drawing that characterizes the edge of a form. In "blind" contour drawing, an artist slowly draws each curve on the edges of an object without looking at the paper.

Contour lines: Lines that define the edges, ridges or outline of a shape or form.

Contrast: A principle of design where light colours are used next to dark colours.

Cool colours: These are the colours that seem to retreat into the background or distance such as green, blue and purple. Colours often associated with cool places, things or feelings.

Elements of design: Colour, line, texture, shape and form.

Focal point: The area in an artwork that attracts the viewer's eye as the centre of interest.

Foreground: The part of the picture plane which appears closest to the viewer and in front of other objects. The foreground is often at the bottom of a picture.

Form: An element of design describing a three-dimensional object.

Foreshortening: A technique used in perspective to produce the illusion of an object retreating into the background.

Horizon line: A level line where water or land seems to end and the sky begins.

Hue: Another word for colour.

Line: An element of design that is used to define shape, contours and outlines. Different lines can suggest a variety of ideas, movements and moods.

Logo: A visual symbol that identifies a business, club, individual or group.

Middle ground: The part of a picture that seems to be in the middle of the picture plane.

Mixed media: Any artwork which uses more than one medium.

Monochromatic: Made using different shades and tints of one colour.

Organic shape: Non-geometric or free-flowing shape.

Perspective: The technique used to represent a three-dimensional world (what we see) on a two-dimensional surface (a piece of paper or canvas) in a way that looks realistic. Perspective is used to generate an illusion of space and depth on a flat surface

Pattern: Lines, colours or shapes repeated in a planned way.

Pointillism: A technique of painting, commonly attributed to Georges Seurat, in which tiny dots of colour are placed close together. From a distance, the dots seem to disappear and the colours blend.

ART GLOSSARY

Primary colours: The basic colours—red, blue and yellow—from which all other colours can be mixed.

Secondary colours: The colours produced by mixing equal amounts of any two primary colours: blue and red produce purple, yellow and red make orange, and blue and yellow make green.

Sgraffito: A technique created by scratching into paint to reveal the colours underneath.

Shade: Dark value of a colour made by adding black.

Shape: An element of design describing the outer form or outline of an image created using line, value, colour and/or texture. Shapes may be geometric or organic, positive or negative.

Sketch: A quick drawing that is used as a reference or plan for an artwork.

Space: An element of design that describes the area around, within or between images or other elements of design.

Still life: An artwork depicting a grouping of inanimate objects.

Subject: A topic or idea represented in an artwork.

Symmetry: Symmetry is demonstrated when portions of the object on opposite sides of a line of symmetry are mirror images one of the other.

Tertiary colours: Colours produced by mixing primary colours with secondary colours.

Tint: Light value of a colour made by adding white.

Texture: An element of design describing the surface quality of an object.

Wash: Created by adding water to paint, making it thin enough to allow colours applied underneath to show through.

Warm colours: Warm colours are used to make an object seem to advance into the foreground. Red, yellow and orange are warm colours. They suggest warm places, things and feelings.

Value: The lightness or darkness of a colour.

Vanishing point: In linear perspective, a position on the horizon where lines or rays between near and distant places appear to come together.

SUPER ARTIST

_____

Keep it up!

ARTIST SUPERSTAR!

_____

GREAT ART!